EGMONT
We bring stories to life

First published in Great Britain in 2016 by Egmont UK Limited,
The Yellow Building, 1 Nicholas Road, London W11 4AN

Written by Katie Westlake
Designed by Jeannette O'Toole

© 2016 Disney Enterprises, Inc.

ISBN 978 1 4052 8349 6
63786/2
Printed in Italy

Parental guidance is advised for all craft and colouring activities.
Always ask an adult to help when using, glue, paint and scissors.
Wear protective clothing and cover surfaces to avoid staining.

Stay safe online. Egmont is not responsible
for content hosted by third parties.

This **Frozen Annual**
belongs to:

....

Write your name here

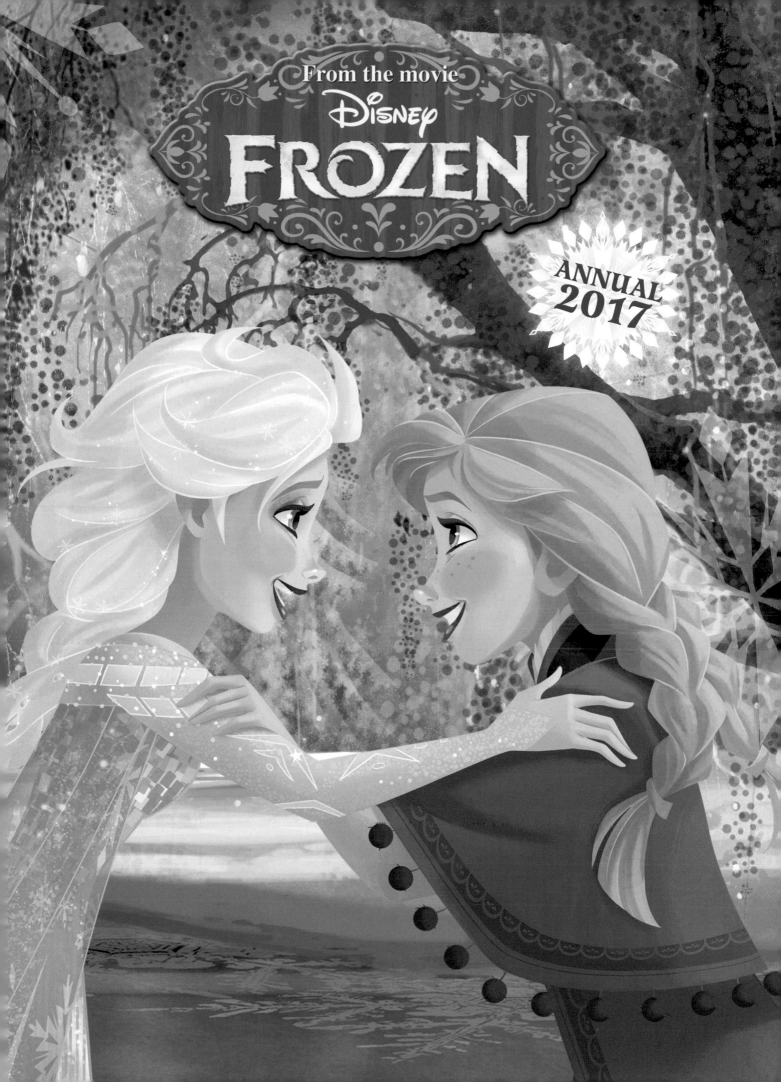

Contents

Frozen Friends

Queen Elsa

Elsa was born with icy powers that can sometimes be difficult for her to control. At first she thought it was better to protect others by keeping her distance, but with a little help from Anna, Elsa realised that love was the key to understanding her magic.

Princess Anna

Princess Anna is a fun-loving optimist, who is always up for an adventure. Anna used to feel lonely but when she discovered her older sister's secret, Anna's big heart was the only thing that could save the kingdom.

Marshmallow

Marshmallow was created by Elsa to guard her ice palace. Although he looks menacing, he is very loyal to Elsa. Despite his scary spikes and loud roar, Olaf named him Marshmallow.

Kristoff

Kristoff is an ice harvester who was raised by Trolls. He used to live alone in the mountains with his only friend, a reindeer called Sven. Kristoff is hardworking, tough and lives by his own rules.

Sven

Sven is Kristoff's loyal reindeer helper. Even though Sven doesn't speak, he always helps Kristoff to do the right thing. He loves eating carrots and is great at pulling a sleigh.

Olaf

Olaf is a curious little snowman with a sunny personality. He loves warm hugs and he's crazy about summer. Elsa created him with her winter magic and gave him his own personal flurry, so he doesn't melt in the sun.

Welcome to Arendelle

Anna welcomes you to her wonderful castle in Arendelle, where she and her sister Elsa grew up.

Where is it?

Replace each of the letters below with the letter that comes after it in the alphabet to find out where the castle lies.

E I N Q C

___ ___ ___ ___ ___

Answer is on page 67.

Home Sweet Home

Join Elsa and discover the colours of the castle when it snows.
Trace the castle then colour it in using the picture below as a guide.

Royal Reflection

Elsa is busy preparing for coronation day.

Spot five differences between Elsa and her reflection in the mirror.

Can you match the character to their shadow?

1

2

3

a

b

c

Answers are on page 67.

Princess Crown

Follow the instructions to make yourself
a crown fit for Elsa's coronation!

You will need:
Card
Scissors
Sticky tape
Crayons or
colouring pencils

1 Ask an adult to help you cut out a piece of
card long enough to wrap around your head.
If you don't have a piece of card big enough,
stick two pieces of
card together.

2 Cut triangles all along one edge of the card
to make the crown shape. Make the crown
as big or as small as you like, you can cut the
crown into different shapes to make a tiara
if you prefer.

3 Decorate your crown using crayons or
colouring pencils. You can add feathers,
stickers or coloured paper too if you wish.

4 Stick together the
two ends of your
crown with sticky
tape. Now your
crown is ready for a
royal outing!

FROZEN

In the kingdom of Arendelle lived two young princesses called Elsa and Anna. Ever since she was born, Elsa had been able to create ice and snow with her magical powers. The sisters loved to play together, but one night, Elsa accidentally struck Anna with her powers.

The king and queen rushed Anna to see the magical Trolls who lived in the mountains. Grand Pabbie Troll cured Anna using his magic, but he had to take away all Anna's memories of Elsa's powers.

"Do you want to build a snowman?"

"Don't worry, I'll leave the fun."

When they were back in Arendelle, the king and queen tried to keep Elsa's magic a secret from everyone, even Anna. They asked Elsa to hide her powers and they locked the castle gates.

Elsa stopped playing with her sister to protect her from harm. As the sisters grew up, Anna was lonely and couldn't understand why her sister didn't want to spend time with her anymore.

When Elsa turned 21, she was crowned Queen of Arendelle. People travelled from all over the kingdom to attend her coronation. Anna was excited as they would finally open the castle gates.

During the celebrations, Anna met Hans, a kind and handsome prince from the Southern Isles. They decided to get engaged right away, but Elsa didn't want Anna to marry someone she had only just met. She told Anna that she wouldn't allow the marriage.

Anna kept arguing until Elsa got angry. With a frustrated wave of her hand a blast of icy magic shot out. Everyone was shocked and terrified. Elsa ran from the castle and went into the mountains to hide away, so she could keep her kingdom safe.

"Will you marry me?"

"ENOUGH!"

At last, Elsa was free to use her powers. When she reached the top of the North Mountain, Elsa created a magnificent ice palace so she could live in peace, without hurting anyone.

Meanwhile in Arendelle, everyone was worried. The kingdom had been plunged into an eternal winter. Anna left Prince Hans in charge, and set off to bring Elsa home. On her way up the mountain Anna met Kristoff, an ice harvester covered in snow. Kristoff and his reindeer friend Sven agreed to help Anna find Elsa.

"The cold never bothered me anyway!"

Anna, Kristoff and Sven made their way up the mountain in Kristoff's sleigh. The journey was difficult and they were chased by hungry wolves! They managed to escape by jumping over a gorge, but they lost the sleigh and had to continue their journey on foot.

As they got closer to Elsa's ice palace, Anna and her new friends looked in amazement at all the beautiful things that Elsa had made with her magic. They met a happy little snowman called Olaf. When Anna explained they were trying to bring back summer, Olaf promised to help her melt the snow. He had never seen summer and couldn't wait to relax in the warm sun.

Olaf took Anna, Kristoff and Sven to the ice palace to talk to Elsa. Anna explained that since Elsa had left, Arendelle was trapped in an eternal winter! Anna begged her sister to come back and melt the snow.

"I like warm hugs!"

"Arendelle's in deep, deep, deep, deep snow."

17

"You belong in Arendelle."

"So do you."

Elsa didn't know how to melt the ice and snow. Angry and upset that she was harming the people of Arendelle, Elsa accidentally struck Anna in the chest with an icy blast. Frightened that she would hurt Anna again, Elsa made a huge snowman to chase them away.

When the friends reached the bottom of the mountain, they realised that Elsa's magic was slowly freezing Anna's heart! Kristoff knew his friends, the Trolls, could help.

Back in Arendelle, Hans had gathered a search party to look for Anna. They made their way up the mountain until they reached the ice palace. Hans captured Elsa and took her back to Arendelle.

Up in the mountains, Kristoff took Anna to see the Trolls. But because the magic had struck Anna's heart, Grand Pabbie couldn't help her.

"Only an act of true love can thaw a frozen heart."

Anna thought that true love's kiss could save her, so Kristoff rushed her back to Hans, but Hans would not kiss her. He just wanted the kingdom for himself! Hans left Anna locked in a room in the castle. Anna was getting colder and colder, soon she would turn to ice. Just when Anna was about to lose all hope, Olaf unlocked the door and helped her escape.

"Please ... help."

"I tried to save her ..."

In the dungeon, Elsa used her icy powers to break her chains and ran away onto the fjord. Hearing of her escape, Hans chased her. He tried to trick Elsa, and shouted after her that Anna had been frozen by Elsa's icy power.

"... but it was too late."

Anna was horrified to see Hans catching up with her sister – she was determined to save her. She threw herself between them before Hans could bring down his sword. Suddenly Anna turned to ice and the sword shattered, breaking into pieces.

When Elsa saw what her magic had done, she threw her arms around Anna and cried. She had never meant for any of this to happen!

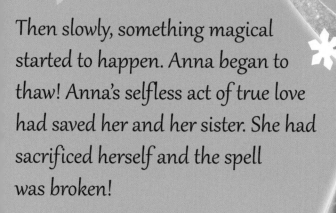

Then slowly, something magical started to happen. Anna began to thaw! Anna's selfless act of true love had saved her and her sister. She had sacrificed herself and the spell was broken!

Elsa finally realised that the key to understanding her power was love. She was then able to bring summer back to Arendelle.

"Love. Of course."

Olaf was so excited to see the summer, but he started to melt. Elsa quickly made a little snow cloud just for him, so he would stay a frosty snowman all year round.

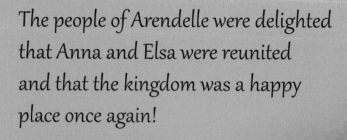

"My own personal flurry!"

The people of Arendelle were delighted that Anna and Elsa were reunited and that the kingdom was a happy place once again!

THE END

Cool Quiz

Are you a *Frozen* fan?
Answer these questions and add
up your score to find out.

1 Which princess has the power to control ice and snow?

a  b

2 Who proposed to Anna after only knowing her less than a day?

a  b

3 Who created the ice palace on the North Mountain?

a  b

4 Who did Anna leave in charge of Arendelle?

a  b

5 Who agreed to help Anna find her way into the mountains?

a  b

6

Who did Elsa create to chase Anna away from the ice palace?

a  b

7

Who was trying to take the kingdom for themselves?

a  b

8

Whose act of true love saved both sisters and the kingdom?

a  b

FINAL SCORE:

4 – 6

You are well on your way to being a *Frozen* super fan.

0 – 3

Why don't you watch the film and read the story again!

7 – 8

Well done! You know pretty much everything there is to know about *Frozen!*

Find Elsa

Anna is looking for Elsa! Find a friend, a dice and two counters so you can help her search.

HOW TO PLAY
Place your counters at the START. Take turns to throw the dice and see who finds her first!

12

11

10

START

9

1

If you stop to play ... miss a turn.

If a troll helps you ... move on two spaces.

If a snowman chases you ... go back two spaces.

8

2

3

5

7

4

6

TIP:
You can use buttons or coins for counters.

13

14

15

16

17

18

28

27

26

19

20

21

Well Done!

29

25

30

24

23

22

FINISH

25

Icy Magic

Can you spot which two snowflakes are identical? Then count how many of each colour snowflakes there are and write the number in the coloured boxes below.

 Blue

 Purple

White

Answers are on page 67.

Show Your True Colours

Colour in this picture of Elsa unleashing her winter magic.

Frosty Hideaway

Elsa has created a spectacular ice palace.
Can you spot the below close-ups in the big picture?

Answer is on page 67.

The North Mountain

Help Anna, Kristoff, Sven and Olaf find their way up the North Mountain. Guide them through the maze by following the snowflakes that match the purple one at the start.

FINISH

START

Answer is on page 67.

Grizzly Guard!

Marshmallow isn't as fierce as he looks! Colour in his icy fingers to finish the picture below.

X	X	X	E	X
X	X	X	X	X
X	L	X	X	X
X	X	X	S	X
X	X	A	X	X

Who is this giant snowman guarding? Cross out every 'X' in the box below to reveal the letters, then write them on the lines below.

___ ___ ___ ___ ___

There are five differences between the two pictures below.
Colour in a circle each time you find one.

Answers are on page 67.

Eternal Winter

Elsa's magic has covered Arendelle in deep snow. Look closely at the picture and try to remember the details. When you are ready, cover the picture and try to answer the questions below.

Greetings from **Arendelle!**

1 Is Anna's cloak pink or blue?

2 Is Kristoff wearing a hat?

3 What colour is Olaf's nose?

4 What is Olaf doing?

a ☐ sliding   b ☐ sitting   c ☐ swimming

5 What is Sven doing?

a ☐ crying   b ☐ sleeping   c ☐ smiling

Answers are on page 67.

Frozen Wordsearch

Help Elsa learn the key to controlling her powers by finding the words hidden in the wordsearch. Colour in a snowflake when you find each one.

G	L	U	S	K	I	Y	M
M	A	G	I	C	A	W	E
Q	N	R	S	P	X	H	S
S	N	M	T	R	U	E	T
L	A	P	E	H	O	A	L
O	B	Y	R	U	E	R	I
V	C	N	S	Q	M	T	S
E	Q	T	I	K	D	A	F

LOVE   MAGIC

SISTERS   HEART

ANNA   TRUE

Answers are on page 68.

33

The Perfect Birthday

It was the morning of Anna's birthday and Elsa was preparing for the big day ...

When you see these pictures say their names out loud:

 Elsa   Anna    Olaf   Kristoff    Sven

 wanted to throw a special

birthday celebration. woke

 up while and

decorated the courtyard for 's

special party. wanted

the day to be perfect, but

she had a cold.

Every time she sneezed tiny snowmen popped

into the air!  and  didn't notice

that  's sneezing was making lots of

little snowmen. When they reached the

courtyard,  ,  and

were waiting on top of a huge pile

of snowmen! The party was

wonderful and it truly was

a perfect birthday.

The End

35

Sisterly Sequences

Look at the pictures of Anna and Elsa below. Can you work out which picture comes next in each sequence?

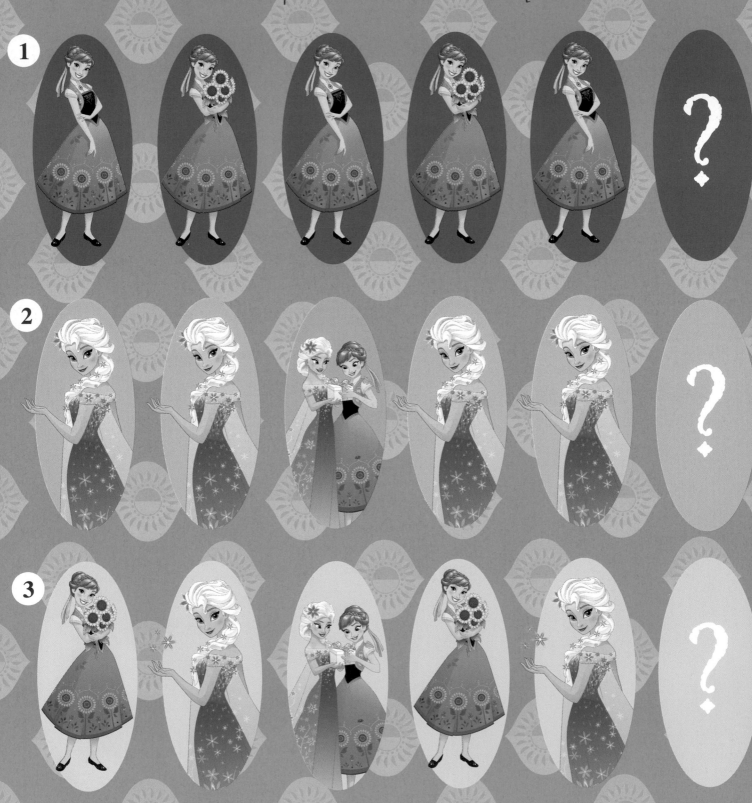

Answers are on page 68.

Party Decorations

Follow the instructions to make some cute decorations.

1 Ask an adult to cut along the dashed line to cut out the strips.

2 Fold one into a loop and use tape or glue to stick the ends together.

© Disney

© Disney

© Disney

© Disney

© Disney

© Disney

© Disney

© Disney

© Disney

37

3 Loop the next strip through it and stick that together.

4 Keep doing this with all the strips until you have a paper chain.

A Pretty Portrait

Anna is having the perfect birthday! Colour her in using the picture as a guide.

Snow Breather

A FAIR IS COMING TO ARENDELLE IN A FEW DAYS AND EVERYONE IS GETTING READY ...

ANNA! I FOUND IT! I KNOW WHAT I WANT TO DO AT THE FAIR ...

... I WILL BE A FIRE-BREATHER!

!

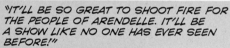
"IT'LL BE SO GREAT TO SHOOT FIRE FOR THE PEOPLE OF ARENDELLE. IT'LL BE A SHOW LIKE NO ONE HAS EVER SEEN BEFORE!"

WELL ... I THINK YOU'D BE GREAT, OF COURSE ...

ME TOO, ANNA.

... BUT MAYBE THINGS WON'T GO EXACTLY AS YOU IMAGINE.

WHY?

WELL ... I THINK ...

I KNOW YOU CAN DO IT, OLAF!

ELSA!

SERIOUSLY? I MEAN ... OF COURSE ... BUT HOW?

Manuscript: Alessandro Ferrari; Layout: Nicoletta Baldari; Cleanup: Nicoletta Baldari; Color: Dario Calabria

IT WON'T EXACTLY BE FIRE BUT IT WILL BE AMAZING, I PROMISE. YOU JUST NEED A LITTLE HELP ...

FSHHH

THIS WILL BE OUR SECRET!

WOW! A GIANT SNOW ... LOLLIPOP!

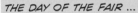

THE DAY OF THE FAIR ...

LADIES AND GENTLEMEN OF ARENDELLE, I'M HAPPY TO PRESENT YOU ...

... OLAF, THE SNOW-BREATHER!

CLAP CLAP CLAP

FSHHH

OLAF KNEW ANYTHING WAS POSSIBLE WHEN YOU HAVE REAL FRIENDS BY YOUR SIDE.

SO BEAUTIFUL!

HURRAY FOR OLAF THE SNOW-BREATHER!

EVEN IF OLAF IS A SNOW-BREATHER AND NOT A FIRE-BREATHER, HE CREATED A SHOW LIKE NO ONE HAD EVER SEEN BEFORE!

The End

Summer Daydreams

Olaf is daydreaming about summer. What activity do you think he is thinking about? Draw it in his thought bubble.

Olaf's Word Jumble

Olaf has his letters all mixed up!
What word is he trying to spell?
Copy the letters into the matching
coloured boxes to find out.

S P N E
N
P R E
E T
S

Party Time for Anna!

Join the party and celebrate Anna's birthday!
Complete the activities below to help Elsa prepare for the big day.

Design some birthday bunting for the party.

Make Anna's birthday invitation. Trace over the dotted letters then colour it in.

You are Invited to

Find the odd Olaf out.

1 **2** **3** **4**

Decorate
the birthday
cake.

Happy
Birthday,
Anna!

Answer is on page 68.

Dance Steps

There's a fun ball at the castle tonight. Finish Anna's gown by finding the missing piece!

a

b

c

d

e

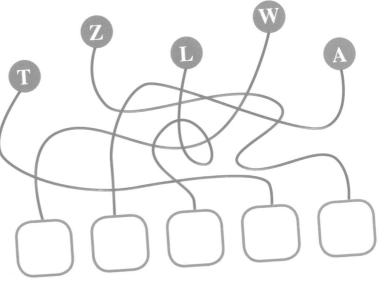

Elsa's Lesson

Follow the trails and write the letters to reveal the name of the dance Elsa wants to learn.

T   Z   L   W   A

A New Dance

Anna's teaching Elsa a new dance. Match each numbered step to the same colour step below. Then write the right number next to it.

START

1

4

2

5

FINISH

3

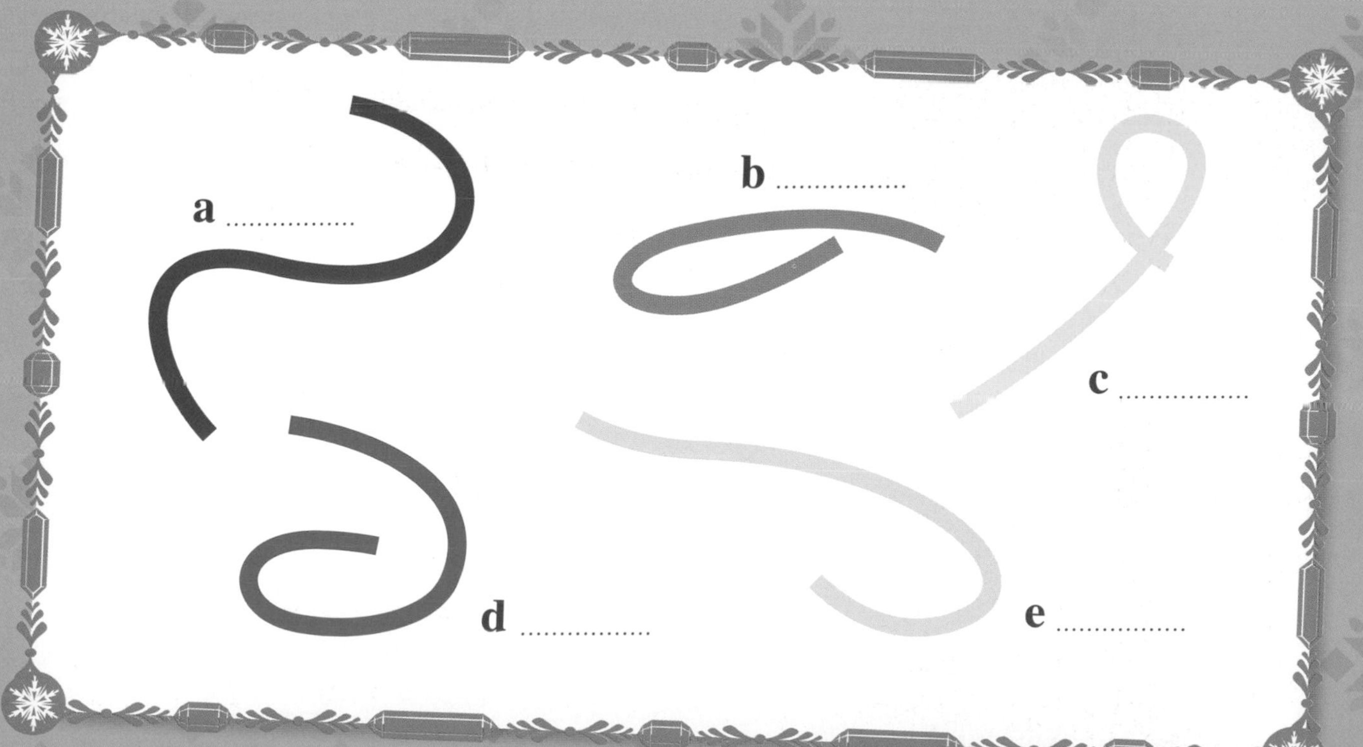

a ....

b ....

c ....

d ....

e ....

Special Gift

Help Kristoff prepare a special gift for Anna. Use these pattern ideas to decorate it.

Secret Present

Colour in the dotted sections to find out what is inside the package.

Manuscript: Alessandro Ferrari; Layout: Elisabetta Melaranci; Cleanup: Arianna Rea, Federica Salfo; Ink: Michela Frare, Cristina Stella; Color: Dario Calabria

IT'S DAWN AT ARENDELLE CASTLE AND STRANGE NOISES ARE WAKING EVERYBODY UP ...

THUMP

CRACK

THUMP

?

WHAT'S THAT?

TAP

THUMP

CRACK

THUMP

SOMETHING IS GOING ON ...

I'D BETTER TAKE A LOOK.

ANNA?!

WHAT ARE YOU DOING?

GOOD MORNING, ELSA!

KRISTOFF IS TEACHING ME HOW TO CLIMB!

IT'S NOT THAT HARD ... I'M DOING **GREAT**! LET'S DO IT **AGAIN** AS SOON AS THIS CLIMB IS FINISHED!

DON'T USE THE **ROPE**, LOOK FOR **HANDHOLDS**!

BE CAREFUL!

DON'T WORRY ELSA, KRISTOFF IS AN **EXPERT**! I'M HAVING A LOT OF **FUN**!

COME ON, ANNA ... YOU MADE IT!

WHOA!

SEE? ISN'T IT **BEAUTIFUL**?

IT'S ... **MAGNIFICENT**! REALLY WORTH IT!

IF I DIDN'T KNOW ANY BETTER, I WOULD CALL IT A PROPER **DATE**, KRISTOFF ...

IT **ISN'T**! WELL ... I MEAN ... IT COULD BE ...

The End

The Right Block

Kristoff always has lots of work to do. Help him gather all of the blocks of ice like the one shown below without going backwards.

How many blocks of ice did you gather for Kristoff?

FINISH

Answers are on page 68.

Such a Deer Friend!

Sven is Kristoff's best buddy! Complete the dot-to-dot below to finish Sven's antlers, then colour him in.

Spot the Difference

There are six differences between these two pictures. Colour in a snowflake each time you spot one.

1

2

Answers are on page 68.

Hidden Name

Can you work out which name is being spelled out?
Write the letter that matches the image in the spaces below.

Answer is on page 68.

Draw a Troll

Even though Trolls are loud and a little bossy, they always want the best for Kristoff and his friends. Copy the below Troll into the box opposite. Use the grid as a guide.

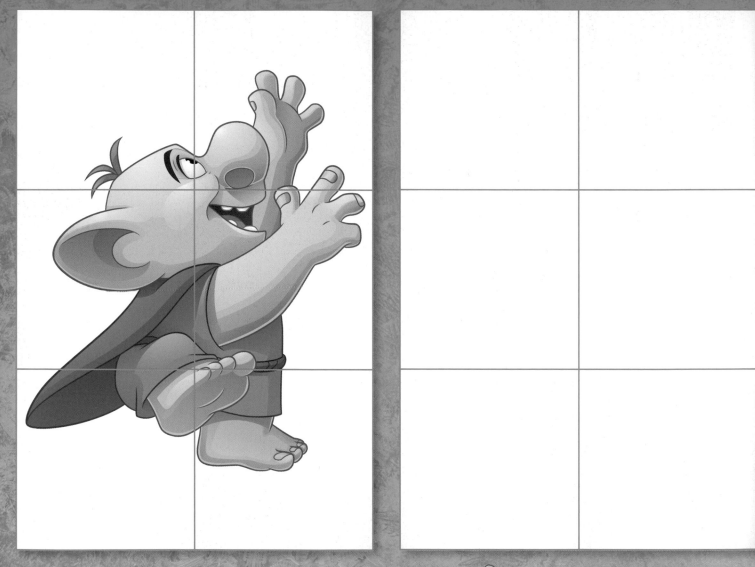

Jigsaw Pieces

Can you find where the jigsaw pieces fit in the pictures below?

Answers are on page 68.

Snowball Champion

A SNOWBALL FIGHT? I'LL WIN!

FSHHH

THUMP

THUMP

THUMP

!

NOBODY CAN BEAT AN ICE HARVESTER!

YOU SPOKE TOO SOON, ELSA!

HA! DO YOU REALLY THINK YOU CAN BEAT A SNOWMAN?

THUMP

THUMP

THUMP

!

I'M

THE BEST

SNOWBALL

THROWER

OKAY! OKAY! WE GIVE UP, OLAF! YOU WIN!

EVER!

Manuscript: Alessandro Ferrari; Layout: Nicoletta Baldari; Cleanup: Nicoletta Baldari; Colour: Rosa La Barbera; Colour: Stefania Santi

The End

Carrot Capers!

Olaf lost his nose when he was playing in the snow!
Help him find it before Sven gobbles it up.

FINISH

START

Winter Games

Elsa and Anna love to play together. What's the name of this classic winter game? Follow the paths of each throw and write the letters in the spaces to find out!

N

S

O

Frozen Flurry

Draw some more snowflakes in the sky to create a beautiful snowstorm!

Lost Friends

Find these two friends hiding in the snow!

L

L W

B A

Fight!

Which Frozen Friend Are You?

Answer the questions below and add up your score to find out
which character you are most like.

1 Your friends would describe you as:

a ☐ Adventurous, chatty and optimistic   b ☐ Regal, powerful and a great leader   c ☐ Hard-working, loyal and brave

2 Which of these is the most important to you?

a ☐ Your family   b ☐ Your kingdom   c ☐ Your sleigh

3 Sometimes you can be known to be:

a ☐ A little clumsy   b ☐ A bit stubborn   c ☐ A bit rough around the edges

4 Who would you like to be your best friend?

a ☐ Elsa   b ☐ Anna   c ☐ Sven

5 What is you favourite thing about winter?

a ☐ Warm hugs with your family   b ☐ The snow – the cold never bothered you anyway   c ☐ The ice is good for harvesting

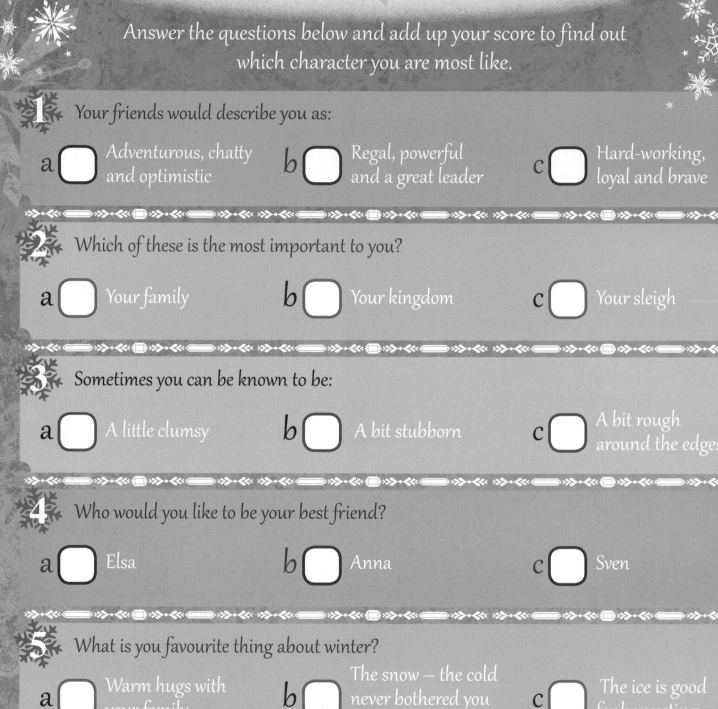

Mostly **a**
Anna

Mostly **b**
Elsa

Mostly **c**
Kristoff

SISTERS

are magic

From the movie
Disney
FROZEN

MAKE EVERY ADVENTURE AMAZING

© Disney

ELSA

QUEEN OF ICE AND SNOW

From the movie
Disney
FROZEN

Anna
MY OWN KIND
OF GRACEFUL!

Answers

Page 10
Welcome to Arendelle
The castle lies in a FJORD.

Page 12
Royal Reflection

1 - b,

2 - c,

3 - a.

Page 22
Cool Quiz
1 - b, 2 - a, 3 - b, 4 - b,

5 - a, 6 - a, 7 - b, 8 - a.

Page 26
Icy Magic

Page 28
Frosty Hideaway

Page 29
The North Mountain
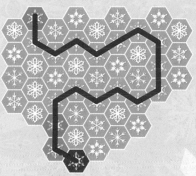

Page 30
Grizzly Guard
ELSA

Page 32
Eternal Winter
1. pink, 2. no, 3. orange,

4. a - sliding, 5. c - smiling.